Do you want to get free children's e-books? Scan the QR code and join the community:

What do I want to be when I grow up?

THIS BOOK BELONGS TO:

_____

Through this lovely coloring book, you will discover and understand amazing careers while having a lot of fun coloring. This is a great opportunity to start important conversations, discover your talents, and start dreaming about your future without limitations.

PHYSICISTS

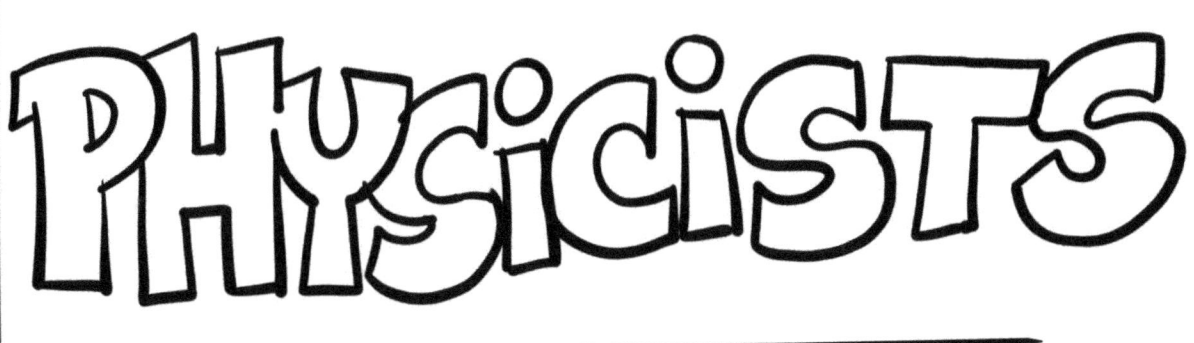

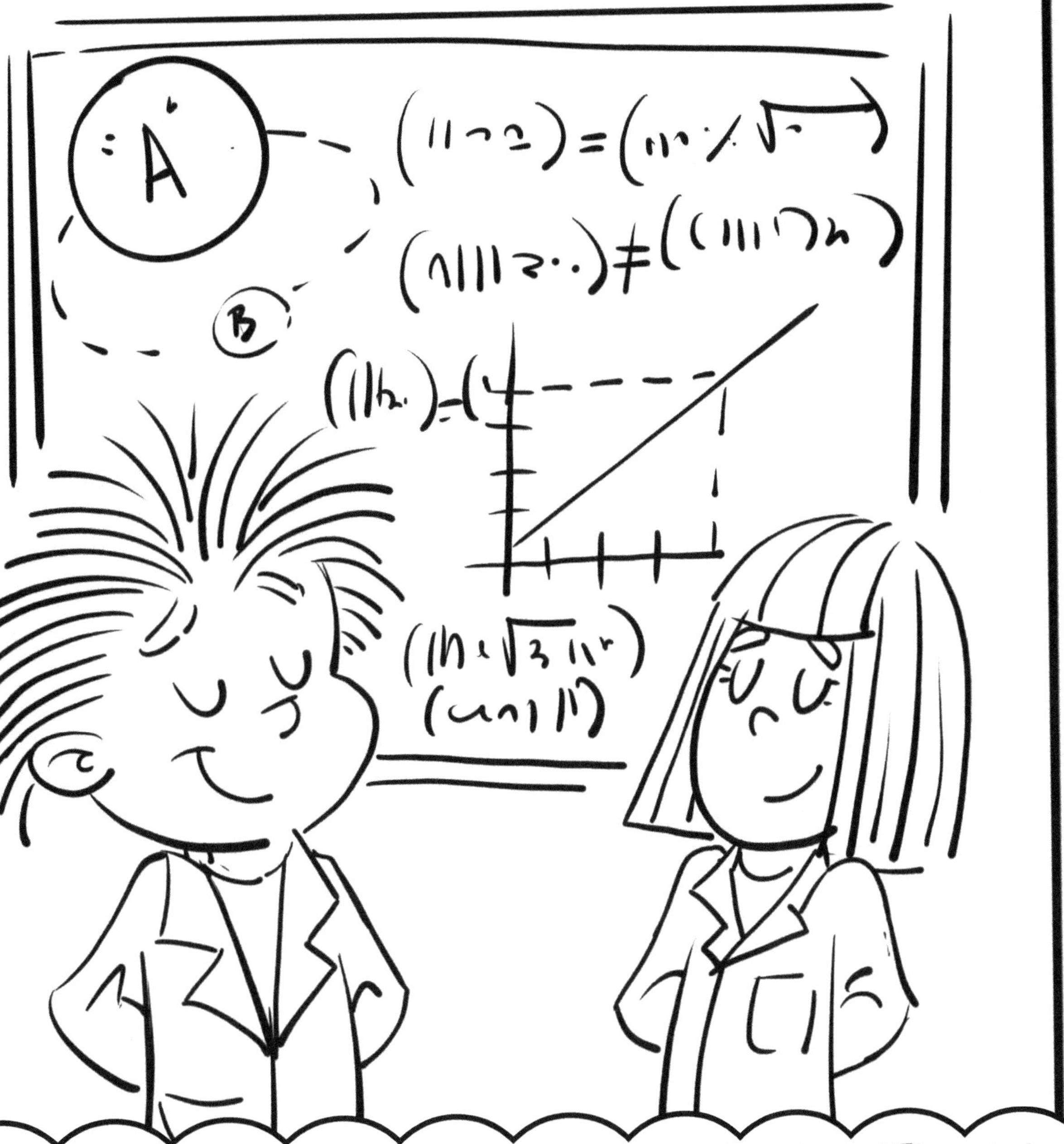

Awesome people who love to explore the secrets of the universe! They study physics, which is a special kind of science that helps us understand everything around us, like how things move, why the sky is blue, and how light works. Physicists are like superhero scientists who use their amazing minds and cool tools to uncover the mysteries of matter and energy!

A special person who is part of the police force and works hard to keep everyone safe. They protect people and their belongings by making sure everyone follows the rules and laws that help our community stay peaceful. Cops are like real-life superheroes who ensure that we can live in a happy and secure neighborhood!

An amazing person with a special medical degree who takes care of people when they are sick or hurt. They use their knowledge and skills to help patients feel better and get healthy again. Doctors are like superheroes in white coats who bring comfort and healing to those in need!

COOK

A talented person who creates delicious meals by preparing and cooking food, just like magic in the kitchen! They have a special skill for combining ingredients and using heat to make our favorite dishes taste incredible. Cooks can be found in restaurants or even at home, making sure our tummies are happy with their tasty creations!

A creative person who dreams up and plans how things should look and work before they are made or built. They use their imagination and draw detailed pictures to bring their ideas to life. Designers are like artistic wizards who make sure everything around us is beautiful and functional, making the world a more amazing place!

JOURNALIST

An incredible storyteller who brings us the latest news and exciting stories! They write articles for newspapers, magazines, or news websites, or prepare news to be shared on TV or the radio. Journalists have a special talent for finding out important information and sharing it with the world. They are like detectives of information, keeping us informed and entertained with their words!

ASTRONAUT

A brave adventurer who has been specially trained to travel in space, exploring the vastness beyond our planet! They journey to the stars and beyond, leaving Earth to discover new worlds and learn amazing things about the universe. Astronauts are like cosmic pioneers, pushing the boundaries of what we know and inspiring us with their incredible space voyages!

A remarkable leader who serves aboard a powerful warship, dedicated to protecting their country's waters and shores. They are brave and skilled individuals who command and guide the ship and its crew to keep their nation safe. Navy officers are like guardians of the sea, working together with their team to ensure the security and defense of their homeland!

WRITERS

Imaginative wordsmiths who create captivating books, stories, and articles to be shared with the world! They have a special talent for crafting words and painting vivid pictures with their writing. Writers work hard to entertain, educate, and inspire readers with their amazing stories and ideas. They are like magicians of the written word, enchanting us with their literary creations!

MICROBIOLOGIST

A curious scientist who explores the hidden world of tiny living things, like bacteria and other microorganisms. They use their special microscope eyes to study these tiny creatures and understand how they live and interact with the world around us. Microbiologists are like detectives of the microscopic world, uncovering the secrets of these fascinating little beings and helping us better understand the wonders of life!

A wise and knowledgeable person who understands the law and helps others navigate it. They are like legal superheroes who study and practice law to give advice and support to people. Lawyers provide guidance and speak on behalf of others in court, making sure everyone's rights are protected and justice is served. They are champions of fairness and defenders of the law!

STATISTICIAN

A clever person who loves working with numbers and using them to uncover important information! They are skilled in collecting, analyzing, and interpreting lots of numerical data to help us understand the world better. Statisticians are like data detectives who uncover hidden patterns and trends, helping us make sense of big numbers and make smart decisions based on the information they find. They are the math wizards who bring order to the world of numbers!

SALESMAN SALESWOMAN

A friendly and helpful person who loves connecting people with the things they need and want! They work in shops or directly with customers to help them find the perfect products. Salespeople have a special talent for listening to what customers want and providing them with the right choices. They are like magical matchmakers, bringing smiles to people's faces by helping them find exactly what they're looking for!

FOOTBALL PLAYERS

Amazing athletes who play the thrilling sport of football, and for some, it's their dream job! They dedicate themselves to the game and get paid to play football professionally. These talented individuals showcase their skills on the field, running, kicking, and scoring goals with incredible teamwork. Football players are like sports superheroes, bringing excitement and joy to fans around the world with their incredible talent and love for the game!

GEOGRAPHERS

Amazing adventurers who specialize in studying and exploring our fascinating world! They dive deep into the landscapes, climates, and connections between people and places. They are like globe-trotting detectives, with the help of maps, tools, and their keen observations, they uncover the secrets of our Earth, revealing its incredible diversity and helping us appreciate the wonders that surround us!

SURGEONS

Skilled doctors who have received special training to perform incredible acts of medical surgery! They have the expertise to use precise tools and techniques to fix and heal the human body. Surgeons work with great care and precision to perform surgeries that help people feel better, heal injuries, or treat diseases. They are like masterful healers with steady hands, using their surgical skills to bring hope and restore health to those in need!

Amazing individuals who delve into the fascinating realm of the human mind, emotions, and behaviors, and how different situations impact us. They carefully study and understand how our thoughts and feelings shape who we are. They explore why we behave the way we do and help us navigate through life's ups and downs. They are like compassionate detectives of the mind, uncovering the mysteries of human behavior and guiding us towards greater understanding and well-being!

TRANSLATORS

Language wizards who have a magical ability to transform words from one language into another! Translators use their expertise to bridge the language barrier, ensuring that messages, stories, and ideas can be shared and understood by people from different parts of the world. They are like linguistic superheroes, bringing people closer together through the power of words!

MANAGERS

Skilled individuals who take charge and lead an organization or a specific department within a company. They are responsible for making sure things run smoothly and that everyone works together towards common goals. Managers use their expertise to make important decisions, solve problems, and support their team members. They are like the captains of a ship, guiding their crew towards success and making sure everything is in order!

MACHINISTS

Skilled individuals who work with machines, either operating them or creating and fixing machinery. They have a special talent for working with tools and equipment, using their knowledge to shape and mold materials into useful objects. Machinists are like mechanical magicians, turning raw materials into precise parts or repairing machines to keep them running smoothly. They play a vital role in manufacturing and engineering, bringing our mechanical creations to life!

MUSICIANS

Talented individuals who have a gift for playing music, bringing beautiful melodies and rhythms to life! They are skilled in playing instruments, singing, or creating music using their voices or electronic tools. Musicians use their creativity and passion to express emotions and captivate our hearts. They are like maestros of sound, filling the world with harmonies that inspire, entertain, and touch our souls!

FINANCIAL ANALYSTS

Smart and analytical experts who evaluate the financial health of businesses or assets to help decide if they are good investments. They carefully examine numbers, data, and economic trends to provide valuable insights and recommendations. Financial analysts are like financial detectives, investigating and analyzing to help investors make informed decisions and maximize their financial success. They are the financial superheroes who navigate the world of money and guide us towards smart financial choices!

OLYMPIC ATHLETIC TRAINERS

Dedicated healthcare heroes who specialize in caring for athletes before, during, and after the Olympic Games. They focus on preventing, assessing, treating, and rehabilitating athletic injuries. These trainers are like guardian angels of the sports world, providing expert care and support to help athletes perform their best and recover from injuries on their Olympic journey!

ELECTRICAL ENGINEER

Brilliant experts who specialize in electrical systems, especially those that power machines and control communication. They possess deep knowledge and skills in designing, analyzing, and improving electrical systems. Electrical engineers are like master architects of electricity, ensuring that our machines work smoothly and that we can communicate effectively. They bring power to our world and connect us through their expertise and innovation!

MODEL

Beautiful individuals who bring fashion and art to life! They pose for artistic photo shoots, showcasing clothing and accessories in stunning pictures. Models also grace the runway during fashion shows, strutting with style and elegance. They are like living canvases, inspiring designers and photographers with their grace and poise. Models add glamour and creativity to the world of fashion, making it a visual masterpiece for all to admire!

LIBRARIANS

Knowledge guardians in libraries, trained to assist and guide us in the world of books and information. They organize materials, offer recommendations, and help us explore the wonders of reading and learning. Librarians are the heroes of the library, opening doors to endless adventures through the power of books!

NURSE
MALE NURSE

Compassionate caregivers who are specially trained to take care of the sick, particularly in hospitals, working closely with doctors. They provide essential support, following the guidance of doctors, to ensure patients receive the best care. Nurses are like caring angels, tending to the needs of those who are unwell, administering treatments, and offering comfort and support. Whether male or female, nurses play a vital role in keeping us healthy and helping us recover. They are true healthcare heroes!

An artistic wizard who brings colors to life on canvas or transforms the world around us with a brush! They are skilled artists who create beautiful pictures using paint and imagination. Painters can also be professionals who paint buildings, walls, and other surfaces, adding vibrant hues and creative designs to enhance our surroundings. Whether they paint on canvas or buildings, painters are like magicians of color, making the world a more vibrant and visually stunning place!

GENETICIST

Scientists trained in the study of genes and heredity—the passing of traits from parents to children. They unlock the secrets of our genetic information, exploring DNA and how it shapes who we are. Geneticists are like genetic detectives, uncovering the mysteries of inheritance and advancing our understanding of genetics. They are the heroes of the genetic code, revealing the wonders of our existence!

PERSONAL TRAINER

Fitness experts who create customized exercise programs for individuals, motivating and guiding them to achieve their goals. They are like dedicated coaches, inspiring and supporting their clients on their fitness journey. Personal trainers help improve fitness, build strength, and promote a healthy lifestyle. They are fitness superheroes, unlocking their clients' potential!

Historians

Experts who study and write about history, examining specific periods, regions, or social phenomena. They uncover the stories of the past, helping us understand how it has shaped our present and future. Historians are like detectives of history, piecing together its puzzle for us to explore and learn from.

PiLOT

Skilled individuals who take control of aircraft, operating the flying controls with precision and expertise. They are like masters of the skies, guiding planes through the air with confidence and skill. Pilots ensure safe and smooth journeys for passengers, navigating through the clouds and bringing us to our destinations. They are the heroes of aviation, turning dreams of flight into a reality!

ECONOMISTS

Inquisitive individuals who study the relationship between a society's resources and its production or output. They analyze data and patterns to understand how economies work and improve efficiency. Economists are like detectives of wealth, unraveling the secrets of economic growth and guiding us towards prosperity!

DANCERS

Passionate individuals who express themselves through the art of dance, whether professionally or for pure enjoyment. They move gracefully, telling stories and evoking emotions through their fluid movements. Dancers bring joy to themselves and others, captivating audiences with their rhythm and expression. They are like poetry in motion, using their bodies to communicate and inspire us with their extraordinary talent and dedication!

CHEMISTS

Curious scientists who explore the fascinating world of chemistry, studying the properties and interactions of substances. They work with chemicals, conducting experiments and analyzing their reactions to uncover the secrets of matter. Chemists are like wizards of molecules, unlocking the building blocks of our world and developing new materials and solutions. They are the heroes of the lab, constantly seeking knowledge to improve our understanding of the world around us!

ACCOUNTANT

Diligent number wizards who keep track of money and financial records for companies or individuals. They meticulously record and analyze the money received, paid, and owed, ensuring accuracy and compliance with financial regulations. Accountants are like financial detectives, uncovering the story behind the numbers and helping businesses and individuals make informed financial decisions. They are the guardians of financial integrity, ensuring that finances are in order and businesses can thrive!

DETECTIVES

Skilled investigators who specialize in uncovering information about crimes and identifying those responsible for them. They work tirelessly to gather evidence, analyze facts, and follow leads to solve mysteries and bring justice. Detectives are like real-life Sherlock Holmes, using their keen observation, critical thinking, and problem-solving skills to piece together the puzzle of a crime. They are the heroes of justice, working to keep communities safe and ensure that the truth prevails!

CIVIL ENGINEER

Architects of infrastructure who plan and build public structures like buildings, roads, bridges, and more. They create blueprints and oversee construction, shaping our physical environment. Civil engineers are master builders, connecting communities and improving our world! Civil engineers are the heroes of construction, making our world a better place!

CAR RACER

Skilled drivers who compete in thrilling races, such as Formula 1 car racing. They possess exceptional driving abilities, maneuvering high-speed vehicles with precision and expertise. Car racers live for the adrenaline rush, pushing the limits of speed and skill on the track. They are like modern-day daredevils, captivating audiences with their thrilling performances. Car racers are the heroes of the racecourse, chasing victory and embodying the spirit of fast-paced competition!

BUSINESSMAN
BUSINESSWOMAN

Ambitious individuals who work in the world of business, including those in high-ranking positions within companies. They are like captains of industry, leading and making strategic decisions to drive success. Business people are adept at managing resources, analyzing markets, and building relationships. They are driven by innovation and the pursuit of growth, contributing to the economy and creating opportunities. They are the heroes of commerce, shaping industries and making an impact in the business world!

Animal doctors who are trained and authorized to provide medical care for animals. They diagnose and treat illnesses and injuries, ensuring the well-being of our beloved pets and wildlife. Veterinarians are the guardians of animal health and welfare, dedicated to keeping animals happy and healthy!

TEACHER

Dedicated individuals who educate and inspire students, especially in schools. They possess a passion for sharing knowledge and helping students grow academically and personally. Create engaging lessons, foster a positive learning environment, and provide guidance and support to their students. They are like mentors and guides, nurturing young minds and shaping the future. Teachers are the heroes of education, empowering students to reach their full potential and make a difference in the world!

SOFTWARE DEVELOPER

Skilled individuals who design, build, and maintain software using various tools and coding languages. They are the architects of the digital age, transforming ideas into functional applications. Software developers shape the way we interact with technology, constantly adapting to meet evolving needs. They are the magicians of the digital world, enchanting us with their coding expertise!

Talented individuals who professionally use their voices to captivate audiences through the art of singing. They bring joy and connect with people through the power of music. Singers are the stars of the stage, sharing their unique voices and touching hearts with their beautiful melodies!

JUDGE

Respected individuals who oversee trials, make legal decisions, and determine punishments. They ensure fairness and uphold justice in the legal system, considering evidence and arguments before reaching verdicts. Judges are the guardians of the law, protecting rights and maintaining order in the court.

Skilled individuals who bring characters to life on stage, in movies, or on television. They dedicate themselves to the craft of acting, captivating audiences with their performances. Actors and actresses express emotions, tell stories, and transport us into different worlds through their talent and versatility. They breathe life into scripted roles, immersing themselves in the art of portrayal.

DENTIST

Qualified individuals who diagnose and treat dental diseases and conditions, focusing on the health of teeth and gums. They help patients maintain oral well-being through examinations, treatments, and guidance on dental care. Dentists are dedicated to ensuring healthy smiles and promoting optimal oral health.

Professionals who design and oversee the construction of buildings. They create innovative designs and ensure that structures are built correctly, considering aesthetics, functionality, and safety. Architects shape the physical spaces we inhabit, combining creativity and technical expertise to bring visions to life. They are the visionary creators behind the buildings that define our world.

The top leader in a company or institution, responsible for making important decisions and providing overall leadership. They set goals, guide teams, and ensure the success of the organization. They bear the ultimate responsibility for the organization's performance and its impact on stakeholders. The CEO is the visionary leader, steering the company towards its objectives and inspiring others to achieve greatness.

Thank you very much for your order! There are many options, but you chose us and that means a lot.

Thank you very much for your support!

GRATITUDE, LOVE, AND BLESSINGS TO YOU AND YOUR FAMILY!